WORDS OF THOUGHT

TANAYA BHALERAO

Copyright © Tanaya Bhalerao
All Rights Reserved.

This book has been published with all efforts taken to make the material error-free after the consent of the author. However, the author and the publisher do not assume and hereby disclaim any liability to any party for any loss, damage, or disruption caused by errors or omissions, whether such errors or omissions result from negligence, accident, or any other cause.

While every effort has been made to avoid any mistake or omission, this publication is being sold on the condition and understanding that neither the author nor the publishers or printers would be liable in any manner to any person by reason of any mistake or omission in this publication or for any action taken or omitted to be taken or advice rendered or accepted on the basis of this work. For any defect in printing or binding the publishers will be liable only to replace the defective copy by another copy of this work then available.

My Son Mst. Samarth Sharad Bhalerao

Lakhamapur

Contents

Contents

Contents

Preface

Introduction of Book

It gives me great pleasure in words of thought book for all. This book is written taking consideration the need of thoughts in this modern Era. It is very effective means of self-expression. It is harmonious blending of creative thoughts. It does not come automatically but it can be acquired by experience.

I hope that this book will be immensely useful for all to get life better.

Thanks.

- Tanaya Bhalerao

Acknowledgements

I want to thank Respected Dr. Sudhir Deore Sir for editing this Book. Sir gives the most valuable finishing touch to the conents penned by me and performed an important role in this book also.

Thank you so much KDB Institute of Lakhamapur, My Husband Sharad Bhalerao.

Thanks to Mr. Vikas Sonawane (Prof of K.D.B.), Mr. Nazim Khan (Prof of K.D.B.), Mr. Manohar Dhamane (Lect of K.D.B.) all staff of KDB.

Also thanks to Book cover artist Darshana Kolge and Notion Press Publication, Chennai.

Thanks my Mother and Father.

Thanking you again.

- Tanaya Bhalerao
Principal of KDB School
Lakhamapur - 423213

***

Words of Thought : Tanaya Bhalerao
Cover : Darshana Kolge
Publication : Notion Press, Chennai
First Edition : 27 June 2022

1

When all are around us,

sometimes we don't value them.

If they are not around us,

we realize their value.

2

Thought

Home is a living

Platform

Of human being

3

Thought

Lives need society for

satisfaction,

motivation,

to see beauty of nature,

to stand, to raise,

giving taking process.

4

Thought

Family without children is as,

courtyard without plants.

♡♡♡

5

Thought

Loneliness is the biggest

punishment for human.

6

Thought

God is

Generator,

Operator,

Destroyer.

7

Thought

When good time,

All are with us.

When bad time,

Few are with us.

All means public,

Few means

Our wellwisher.

8

Thought

Communication is a lifeline of

any relation. As you stop

communicating, you initiate to

lose valuable relation.

9

Thought

Mind, Body, Soul needs energy

for development; A like a car's

engine needs oil for smoothness.

❥❥❥

10

Thought

When we fall ill.

then we realize the importance

of family.

ᗡᗡᗡ

11

Thought

Mother is place

Where Universe

is there.

12

Thought

She can't express her love ,she is

simple,She has love in Her heart

without her blessings life is,

incomplete. She is MOTHER.

13

Thought

Love does'nt

means

two body,

Love means bonding

Between two

mind/soul.

14
Thought

Without kids,

There is no home.

Without kids,

There is no true love.

Without kids,

There is no garden.

Without kids,

There is no voice.

Without kids,

There is not value of parents.

Without kids,

There is no teaching,

Learning process.

❧❧❧

15
Thought

Mental ailment

is dangerous than

physical one.

16

Thought

Happiness,sorrow are

Sides of one coin

If happiness,

Then value of sorrow

If sorrow,

Then value of happiness.

17

Thought

Freedom of Expression

leads to aim achievement.

18

Thought

for marital woman husband

should give freedom to

implement her skill.

19
Thought

Good, better, best.

Never go for rest.

♡♡♡

20

Thought

Better personality

Means

To prove your

quality.

21

Thought

Bonding of two minds should be

from either side not from one

side.

22

Thought

Feelings are the precious gift by

God, preserve it!

♡♡♡

23
Thought

❥

Faith is good,

Blindfaith

isn't good.

♡♡♡

24

Thought

—♡—

We can achieve

Our goal by

Hardwork,

Dedication,

Consistency.

♡♡♡

25

Thought

❤

Creating ideas can

Be possible only

by creative mind.

❤❤❤

26

Thought

Love is judge

Only in difficult

Situation.

27

Thought

We can get

real people in

difficult situation.

ppp

Those thing

We get late,

That's important

Too much.

29

Thought

GOD; an invisible invincible

power. We can feel and

experience but can't see it.

30

Thought

They kick you out, once 'up their

need of you!

♡♡♡

31

Thought

Society is very

Important for living

our life.

32

Thought

Some people kick by

Frontside,

Some people kick by

Backside.

33

Thought

Those people who are

dependent on you, all are not

good.

34

Thought

Prayers give us powerful energy,

so we have to do daily meditate

in front of God statue.

35

Thought

We get

Positive vibes,

If we

Think & implement

Positively.

36

Thought

Though we have freedom but,

we still limitedly dependent on

God!

♡♡♡

37

Thought

———♡———

Birds can fly

in the sky.

Boys can do

anything

at anytime.

♡♡♡

38

Thought

If a bird sits on a branch of a tree

then, it has belife on it's wings

and not on branch of a tree,

because, if we cut the branch, the

bird flies.

ᗡᗡᗡ

39

Thought

Find the unique quality within

and implement it correctly to get

successful.

40

Thought

❦

Age doesn't matter

For any work.

If we have

Will power,

We can do it.

♡♡♡

41

Thought

We have give

100% to work out

nothing

is impossible.

♡♡♡

42

Thought

Once asked to pot

Why do you

Remained cool in

every situation,

Pot answered,

I am made up of mud,

I shall returned to mud,

So,why shall

Pride & Anger ?

ᗡᗡᗡ

43

Thought

Positive thoughts

Convert into

Positive energy.

44

Thought

Continuous study makes us

knowledge

Powerful.

45

Thought

Sickness resides with; ill: mind,

body and soul!

♡♡♡

46

Thought

Mother is most

important person,

You may not purchase it.

It gives you

Immense strength to live,

So,love her mindly,

not physically.

47

Thought

Communication

makes our skill

well develop.

♥♥♥

48
Thought

When you miss your mother; call

her, talk to her, laugh with her,

and see her photos! Love her

unconditionally.

❥❥❥

49

Thought

Don't affection/love

to anyone more,

It will give

you pains.

ꕥꕥꕥ

50

Thought

Teacher should

Keep distance

Physically and

Ideological

Towards students.

❥❥❥

Biodata

Name : Mrs.Tanaya Sharad Bhalerao
Education : D.Ed. (Mumbai) M.A. B.Ed.
Address : Post : Lakhamapur, Taluka : Satana
District : Nashik
Pin code : 423213
Birth Date : 23-03-1984
Vice Chairman, K. D. Bhalerao Education Society
Post : Principal, K. D. Bhalerao International School &
Jr. College, Lakhamapur
Phone No. 02555-235770
Mob No : 8767464847/ 9890718070